Happy Turkey Day

by Christine Taylor-Butler

"Let me help you," I said to our neighbor, Mrs. Mendoza, as she reached for a can of corn on the top shelf of the grocery aisle. Nearby, my mother was searching the freezer section for a turkey.

"Are you looking forward to celebrating Thanksgiving next week?" I asked.

"Absolutely!" Mrs. Mendoza smiled, but I saw that her basket contained only bread, milk, and cheese.

That night, at dinner, I couldn't take my mind off Mrs. Mendoza and the fact that she hadn't bought any Thanksgiving foods. I felt worried she might be spending her holiday alone. I asked my parents if we could invite her to our Thanksgiving dinner.

"Of course!" they said. Later, I called Mrs. Mendoza, and she quickly accepted our invitation. But she also sounded a bit sad.

"I wish my friends had neighbors like you," she explained. "Many of us are alone, but our homes aren't large enough for holiday dinners. That's why we usually spend Thanksgiving by ourselves."

We said goodbye, but I couldn't help wishing our home was big enough to invite Mrs. Mendoza's friends, too.

Suddenly, I had an idea. Papa was on the City Council. He could ask the council to open the community center for Thanksgiving. We could invite everyone who needed a place to celebrate, and each person could bring a favorite food!

Papa loved the idea. "But, Gabriela, I think you should be the one to present it!"

So the next night, I spoke at the town meeting. I ended by saying, "After all, doesn't everyone deserve to have Thanksgiving dinner with friends?" The council, with smiles on their faces, agreed.

When my family arrived at the community center on Thanksgiving Day, it was already overflowing with people, and platters of food covered long serving tables. In the kitchen, Mrs. Mendoza and her friends were laughing as they warmed the special dishes they had brought.

Later, as we all enjoyed our meal, the mayor stepped up to the microphone. "I just want to thank Gabriela for her wonderful suggestion. I propose we hold Turkey Day here every year!"

Everyone clapped and cheered, and I cheered loudest of all.